DEDICATION

I dedicate this book to

my Lord and Savior,

Jesus Christ,

Who has taught me,

blessed me,

encouraged me

and loved me all the way.

OUR PRAYER IN AGREEMENT

Father God, in the name of Jesus Christ, we bind and break all witchcraft, curses, spells, and powers – and through the Blood of the Lamb – destroy the works of every witch, warlock, wizard, sorcerer and all other powers of darkness.

Through the blood of Jesus Christ we break all their powers — including the influences of witchcraft, evil powers, spells, hexes, vexes, voodoo, hoodoo, roots, potions or any such things — off every person who will read this book. For them also we invoke Psalm 80:18, "so we will not go back from thee: quicken us and we will call upon thy name" so that those who read this book will understand, remember and apply consistently what they read.

Through the blood of Jesus Christ we also bind up and destroy all their spirit-guides, helps, and shields of these workers of evil, and leave them without any strength – stripped of their evil power and influence.

In the name of Jesus Christ, and by the Blood of the Lamb, we now seal up their powers within themselves, so that they cannot use them on anyone, and that their works might be destroyed, in the hope that their souls might be saved for the glory of God.

Amen...
...Ruth Brown

TABLE OF CONTENTS

PREFACE

"Witchcraft," as defined in *Webster's Dictionary*, is "the power or practice of witches; black magic; sorcery." A "witch" is defined as a woman supposedly having supernatural power by a compact with the devil or evil spirits. A man with such power is called a "warlock."

Often, people have the false assumption that witchcraft refers to someone putting items in your food. But that is not always the case. There are many forms of witchcraft. In some cases, it involves conjuring up demons from hell and dispatching them to churches or individuals to cause envy, strife, and confusion. Spirits of delusion (which will cause a false belief or opinion, meant to mislead; deceive or trick) are a strong tool used in witchcraft.

I've found in my fifteen years of ministry, that a spirit of delusion can destroy a marriage. For example, it will cause suspicion and false accusations to be made by

9

one spouse against the other. In the church, divisions between Pastors and members can result when this spirit is loosed to attack the pastor. Many pastors have been hurt, deceived, misused and had their churches split as a result.

Another form of witchcraft, consists of speaking evil words against someone. Words have life and when evil words are spoken against someone, this can have a negative effect if the person is not fasting and praying. The demons will take those words and launch an attack.

Praying contrary to the will of God concerning someone or their business, is still another form of witchcraft. God doesn't receive such negative prayers, but Satan does. A person may be praying for a new business, and someone else is praying that they won't get it. I believe that's why the Scripture says:

"Let not thy left hand know what thy right hand doeth."
(Matthew 6:3)

It pays to keep the things that the Lord reveals secret until they are manifested in the natural, to keep others from attacking God's will and purpose in your life.

The Lord showed me in a vision, that a group of men were chanting and working witchcraft against a well-known recording artist out of jealousy. I saw spirits being sent to attack him. So, I tried to reach him through one of his brothers, a hairdresser and a dancer, but he never responded. I talked to his employees and told them what God had said. I tried to warn him, but he didn't receive it. Shortly afterwards, I began seeing on television news that all kinds of confusion, strife, and mishaps were coming against him and his entourage. He fell from "Number 1" on the charts to "off" the charts. I wanted to pray with him to destroy the works of darkness. So I prayed for his hairdresser instead, and he received the prayer, and is still being tremendously blessed. So much so, in fact, that he is now writing a book about this testimony.

Recently, I was working with a men's home in Oakland, praying with the brothers there and working deliverance. The brothers were progressing well in the Lord, until a new man moved into the home. I discerned an occult spirit in his eyes. From the moment he came into the home, all kinds of confusion, envy, and strife began erupting daily.

I approached the man and prayed that blindness, heaviness, and bondage would be destroyed in him and asked God to reveal to him his heart. He then confessed to the Assistant Pastor that he was a wizard ("a male or female magician or sorcerer, one acquainted with the secrets of the unseen world, or an intimate acquaintance

11

of soothsayers;" definition, *Pictorial Bible Dictionary*). He admitted to chanting, but would not repent and turn from his evil deeds. Unbeknownst to him, I was also secretly praying against black magic, and as I did, he started complaining to the counselors that he was going to leave the home. Finally, he did leave and now things are slowly improving there. Prayer will either chase them out or lead to their repentance.

(Remember that people who practice witchcraft are still souls that Jesus died and gave his life for. God loves them and wants them saved, too.)

In this book, I have purposely not disclosed any names in order to protect the privacy and identities of the persons involved. God is my witness that all I have related is the truth.

As an ordained minister for fifteen years, my current ministry is to go into different churches, as led by the Lord, and pray for the work of God there, warfaring against the works of the devil. I love to see people delivered. God has given me a love for fasting and prayer, also.

I love to encourage people because I have made many mistakes in my own early Christian life, and had to seek God diligently for personal deliverance. It is an on-going battle. If you make a mistake or fall short, just repent and seek God for healing and deliverance because He will forgive you and raise you up. People like to condemn, but God forgives. I believe a pure heart is being honest with yourself and it's very important to be honest with God if you're going to be a successful warrior.

God gave me the assignment to write this book to enlighten the Church on the operation of witchcraft, so the body of Christ would not have to suffer these attacks any longer. We have the power through Christ Jesus to destroy these works and to stop them. If one can put a thousand to flight, and two can put ten thousand to flight, just think what the whole body of Christ can do.

It's time for the Church to stop perishing for lack of knowledge. It is also time for those to whom God has already revealed this knowledge, to come forward and tell all, so we can bless one and strengthen one another. Remember, Church, we are all ONE through Christ Jesus, so let's love one another, help one another, and fight with, and not against one another, by fasting and praying and giving God praise at all times. AMEN!

CHAPTER ONE:

PRAYER AND FASTING

When I received salvation, the lady responsible for bringing me to the Lord, advised me to go on a three-day-and-night fast which consisted of zero water and zero food. I thought to myself, "I will die." Since I had no previous experience with the Lord or fasting, I had to ask the question, "Would I die?"

During that time, I had a very strenuous job, driving a forklift and lifting heavy materials, so I asked the lady if this would make it hard for me to fast. She told me that the Lord would take me through it. I went on the fast and it was the hardest thing I had ever done, but the Lord did take me through it.

Shortly after, she told me that I needed to join a church. So, she took me to a church. There was a prophet at that service. (Remember, fasting, as well as "prophets" and the "Holy Ghost" were all new to me, having been a person of the world with a background of drugs and alcohol.)

The prophet didn't even know me, but suddenly he called me out saying, "Young lady, the Lord wants you to go on a three-day fast."

Of course, I didn't want to hear that, so I replied, "I just came off one last week."

"The Lord said to go on a three-day fast, so go on another one," he answered.

Filled with fear of the Lord and excitement about the change in my life - from hate to happiness, and from bondage to freedom, I quickly agreed with him.

I went back on another three-day-and-night fast, totally dry - no food, no water. I was really surprised that this fast was considerably easier than the first one had been. And I found praying was easier while fasting. I said, "Uhm, this fasting and prayer is quite enjoyable, Lord. I'm going to go on a three-day fast each month, just to say thank you for saving me."

The next month came and I went on my three-day fast. In the midst of praying, a nice, peaceful Voice spoke to me, and said to fast three days out of a week. So, I did for about a year. Then, after a year, a Voice spoke to me saying, "Now, go on a forty-day-and-night fast."

I said, "Lord, if this is You, please fix it so I won't have to communicate with my co-workers while I'm on the fast; put me in a new place with people I don't know." And, He did.

16

I was transferred the following week to another building for 90 days, hanging up bin strips and inventory. It was light and easy work. Boy, was I glad. I went on a forty-day-and-night fast drinking only water: nothing else, just water. And, the Lord took me completely through it. Praying was wonderful; there was so much joy. My soul felt like it wanted to burst out of my body and just go on with Jesus.

I'm testifying about this series of fasts because the more I fasted, the more God began to show me things in myself that I didn't like, such as anger, hurt and bitterness. The more I fasted, the more I began to see the real Ruthie. It wasn't a pleasant sight! I spoke to a few Christians about this and asked them what I should do. They tried to make me think that it was all in my mind. This response made me very angry. I assured them that it had nothing to do with my mind.

So, I began to seek the Lord diligently. "Lord, how can I get rid of these things? I don't want to be like this,"

"For that which I do I allow not: for what I would, that do I not; but what I hate, that do I. If then I do that which I would not, I consent unto the law that it is good. Now then it is no more I that do it, but sin that dwelleth in me. For I know that in me (that is, in my flesh) dwelleth no good thing: for to will is present with me; but how to perform that which is good I find not."

(Romans 7:15-18 KJV)

After four-and-a-half years of fasting and praying for the answer, I noticed that the anointing upon me began to grow stronger and stronger. (In 2 Corinthians 1:21, we find that Christians are anointed with the Holy Spirit by God. So the Holy Spirit was getting stronger in my life.) As I prayed for people, they would get healed. Miracles would happen in people's lives. But, still, I had these ugly things in me - in my flesh . . . the anger, hurt and bitterness.

Then, I ran across a book entitled, *"Pigs in the Parlor"* by Frank and Ida Mae Hammond, which opened my eyes. I said, "Lord, this is my answer." In this book, the authors explained that demons come in groups. For instance, hate, bitterness, and anger belong in one group. Lust and perverted spirits belong in another separate group. I came to the understanding that if you're exhibiting one of these demonic personalities, then the others in that group are probably also present.

I began seeking God for revelation knowledge on a system to get these spirits out of me. As I continued to fast and pray, the Lord directed me to "renounce them, to curse the root, to uproot them and command them to leave and return to their own kind, in the name of Jesus." Every time I fasted, I would drive one group out of my flesh through the power of Christ! I began to feel lighter, brighter, and freer. And I noticed that I was beginning to really enjoy fasting.

"Hey, Lord, this is good," I prayed. Fasting got even easier as time went on, and my heavenly language began to flow into deeper intercession and travailing. (Travailing in prayer is intense pain and agony, much like a woman suffering the pains of childbirth.) The Lord Jesus showed me that deep travailing has the effect of a nuclear bomb on the devil, whereas, intercession is like shooting bullets at him. Either way, my fasting was having a tremendous effect.

I began to realize that we are trees of righteousness planted by the rivers of water, and that anger, envy and the like, were dead branches that needed to be pruned from the tree. The more I allowed the Spirit of God to prune me, the more Christ came into me and began to operate in those areas.

> "Every branch in me that beareth not fruit he taketh away: and every branch that beareth fruit, he purgeth it, that it may bring forth more fruit."
>
> (John 15:2 KJV)

When anger left, peace came. When envy left, love came. I became more fruitful. The more Christ came in, the more my flesh died. Then, it became easier to be obedient.

> "For we are his workmanship, created in Christ Jesus unto good works, which God hath before ordained that we should walk in them."
>
> (Ephesians 2:10 KJV)

I'd like to emphasize that fasting and prayer brings submissiveness, along with strength. The combination of the two (fasting and prayer) reveals the true condition of your heart, which is good and necessary. It's good because it allows an individual to see which spirits may be operating against them and through them. And it's necessary because these spirits need to go if we really want to be used greatly by God. If not, Satan will use these weaknesses against us at our weakest moment, and we'll become our own worst enemy.

"Neither give place to the devil."

(Ephesians 4:27)

This Scripture commands us not to give the devil any ground in our lives or a foothold in our soul. If we become aware of these evil spirits working against us, it is our duty to take authority over them in the Name of Jesus and get rid of them by fasting and praying.

"Know ye not that a little leaven leaveneth the whole lump? Purge out therefore the old leaven, that ye may be a new lump, as ye are unleavened."

(I Corinthians 5:6-7)

The Bible gives us many examples in the Old and New Testament to further illustrate this point. One case in point, is the destruction of Samson, one of the mightiest men in the Bible. Samson's unbridled lust for Delilah caused him to betray the Lord and reveal to her the secret of his source of strength. How different Samson's life would have been if he had lived a consecrated life of fasting and prayer.

In the New Testament, Peter lied and denied Christ three times after Christ's arrest. Yet, hours before, he had sworn in Matthew 26:33, *Though all men shall be offended because of thee, yet will I never be offended.* Jesus answered him in the next verse with, *Verily I say unto thee, That this night, before the cock crow, thou shalt deny me thrice.*

Scripture tells us that Peter "wept bitterly" after committing his misdeed. He had a weakness, or flaw in his character, that he was unaware of. But the Lord knew it was there, and He knows what's in us, also. Fasting and prayer will reveal these weaknesses in us and help us to get rid of them.

I can't say enough about fasting and prayer, and its importance in my Christian life. Fasting and prayer helped guide me through many extremely, difficult moments in my life. Fasting made it easier for me to go through trials, as well as able to glorify God in the trials. Remember, Christ in us, is our hope of glory. (Colossians 1:27) Fasting and prayer took me through the confrontations that I've had with the forces of darkness. And throughout these chapters, you will see how fasting and prayer played a great part in overcoming battles.

"Now in the twenty and fourth day of this month the children of Israel were assembled with fasting, and with sackclothes, and earth upon them. And the seed of Israel separated themselves from all strangers, and stood and confessed their sins, and the iniquities of their fathers.

And they stood up in their place, and read in the book of the law of the Lord their God one fourth part of the day; and another fourth part they confessed, and worshipped the Lord their God."

(Nehemiah 9:1-3 KJV)

When I read this, I did pray and ask God to give me a love for fasting. To this day, almost twenty-three years later, I still have a love for fasting.

Father give me a love for Prayer & Fasting

CHAPTER TWO:

CONFRONTATIONS

WITH DARKNESS

In the very first year of my salvation, I was confronted with darkness on four occasions. The first time occurred shortly after being saved. I would regularly call my sister who worked at a liquor store. I'd asked her whether or not her boss was in. Every time that she would say "No," I'd run down to the store and pass out tracts and tell the people how "God so loved the world that He gave His only begotten Son." (This was the only Scripture I knew at that time.) And, I'd tell them how cigarettes and alcohol would destroy their souls. I never had any problems with the people, except for one occasion.

One day, a young man entered the store and began contradicting me. I approached him with my Bible open to show him John 3:16,

"For God so loved the world, that he gave his only begotten Son, that whosoever believeth in him should not perish, but have everlasting life."

As I came within about three feet of him, I looked into his eyes and saw snake heads coming out of the pupils of his eyes. It appeared that worms were crawling around on his face. I shouted, "He's the devil!"

He replied, with a strange voice, "I am sweet Satan." Afterwards, he jumped on his bicycle and rode off.

I turned around to the people and asked them, "Did you see his eyes?"

They said "no," but they had heard what he said. Not too surprising, they all had strange, confused looks upon their faces.

I believe that the Lord let me see this, in order to protect me from getting too close to the young man, for I was then only a month old in the Lord. Being new in the church, I thought that these things always happened. So, I shared the incident with other members of my church. Boy, did I make a big mistake! After I told them, they seemed to be afraid to even shake my hand or get close to me.

I would come home and cry, saying, "Lord, I thought these people were supposed to be full of love." After being rejected by church members over a period of time, I decided to leave that church and go back into the world. I told the Lord my decision, and He instructed me "to stay in Christ." And, I said, "Okay."

Another confrontation happened after I had only been saved for about six months, or a little longer. The pastor asked if I would take a certain woman into my home because she didn't have anywhere else to stay. Still excited about my own salvation, I quickly said, "Yes."

I thought this was the normal, Christian, thing to do. While this person lived with me, the Lord had me going on one fast after another, and praying for hours at a time. I didn't understand at first, I just simply obeyed. During the time she stayed there, a demon began attacking my son. He woke up one night crying, and a voice was speaking out of him, while he was crying. I thought to myself, "It's impossible to cry and to talk at the same time."

The thought flashed into my mind that I should hold my son, look him in the eyes, and say, "Satan, the Lord rebuke you, in the name of Jesus. Come out of him, you devil."

When I did, the demon said, "Okay." Then, my son quieted down and became very peaceful. My son was three years old at that time.

Later, the woman confessed that she was a Satan worshipper, and when she left my home she went on to San Francisco to join the church of Satan. When she left, she took a lot of my possessions with her. To state it plainly, she stole from me. However, because of all the fasting and praying I was doing during the three weeks that she was staying at my house, Satan was not able to carry out his plans through her for my destruction.

I told my pastor about her and she replied, "I knew that something wasn't right about her. That's why I didn't take her into my house."

I thought, thanks a lot. (I don't blame the pastor now, for she was a new pastor at that time.)

The third confrontation with darkness began when a man called me, saying he had an uncashed insurance policy on my mother who had died three years earlier. I went down to his office to see the policy.

This man was hideous looking. Half his face was disfigured. He only had one eye which was red, cold and piercing. I went in, he shut the door, and I proceeded to examine the policy. When I looked at it, I noticed that they had my mother's name spelled wrong.

Then, a voice spoke to me saying, "Get out of there quickly."

I couldn't open the door; it was locked. I turned around and said, "I'm not interested in that policy. Open this door and let me out."

He hesitated. I began to say, "In the name of Jesus, open this door." I repeated this three times, and the third time, he opened the door. I walked out, thanking the

Lord. This was another time that Satan's plan failed. I don't know what this man had planned for me, but it certainly was not good.

The fourth confrontation was just as strange as the others. I always loved to pass out tracts and to witness to people. One day, while passing out tracts, I began witnessing to an older man. He told me that he really didn't have the time, then. But, if I wanted to come by his house and share some Scriptures with him, he'd go over them with me and possibly come to church. He said that he was familiar with the Lord but that he wasn't in the church, at that time.

Young and foolish, I went to his house. Thinking gladly that this would be a soul won back to the Lord, I was fired up to meet with this man. I had my Scriptures and my tracts. I had prayed through before I left home. Man, was I ready!

"Put on the whole armor of God, that ye may be able to stand against the wiles of the devil.
(Ephesians 6:11 KJV)

When I arrived, he had on a white robe, and he invited me into the living room. On the floor, I noticed a circle drawn containing a star with five points, and a candle burning at each of the points. I really didn't know what this meant. So, I assumed that it was harmless.

I sat upon the couch and noticed a table over to my right full of money. In fact, there were several stacks of money on the table. Even with all that money laying on the table, my only interest was for a soul coming to the Lord.

I opened my Bible and said, "Come on, I have my Scriptures. Let's pray and read the Word."

He asked me to step into the circle with him so that I could be his first wife. He said his lord told him that I was supposed to be his first wife and that it was a position of honor. He was to have many wives and I could be number one.

I asked him, "Are you out of your mind?"

I then told him that I was not looking for a husband at that time and even if I were, it certainly would not have been him. He offered the money on the table to me and I told him that I was not interested in his money. My heart was still set on praying and reading the Scriptures, as we had initially agreed. So, I again said, "Let's pray and read the Scriptures."

But he was persistent about me stepping into the circle. It came to me that this was another set up. (Later, a former witch told me that this was a satanic circle.) So, I picked up my Bible and headed for the door. There was no doorknob and the door was locked. At that moment, I started calling on the wonderful name of Jesus and commanding the man to, "Open the door." It took ten minutes of rebuking the devil in him and calling on the name of Jesus before he finally opened the door.

With a great sense of relief, I got out of there. I know that Satan meant bodily and spiritual harm for me, but his plan failed. In my spiritual infancy, I had much zeal and little wisdom, but the Lord was always present to deliver me out of my troubles.

Afterwards, the Scripture, James 1:5 KJV, came to me, *"If any of you lack wisdom, let him ask of God, that giveth to all men liberally, and upbraideth not; and it shall be given him."* I immediately began praying, "Lord, give me wisdom."

During this time, I had no one to counsel me, except for one person who really didn't understand these mysteries. Church members still avoided me because of the first confrontation. I was alone. But this taught me to lean on Jesus and Jesus alone.

It's now twenty-three years later, and I still depend solely on Him. I lean on the Lord to lead me and guide me, as well as to give me instructions in different situations. Believe me, you can't go wrong leaning on Jesus.

Now, I understand why I was instructed at my new birth to go on a three-day-and-night fast, and then, fast after fast, after fast. The Lord knew that Satan had dangerous traps set for me. I had to be obedient and not question the Lord, because He knows everything.

Much fasting and praying set up an anointing to make the devil back off, for every one of his plans fell through. All of these confrontations occurred within the first year of my salvation. I learned how important it was to stay focused on Jesus, and watch out for distractions.

> "Trust in the Lord with all thine heart; and lean not unto thine own understanding. In all thy ways acknowledge him, and he shall direct thy paths."
> (Proverbs 3:5-6 KJV)

It sure would have been nice to have had this Scripture flowing in my heart before that fourth confrontation. Little did I know that all of these circumstances were happening, in order to prepare me for intercessory warfare against witches, warlocks and powers of darkness.

Many people are still unaware of the existence of these evil personalities. They think witches and warlocks are fictional, and belong only to the realm of children's fairy tales. But there are modern-day people practicing witchcraft. These people look normal, but are part of an orchestrated movement to infiltrate and weaken the power of the church. (I discovered that they are even sent to schools to learn how to dance and pray like we do.) They imitate us so closely that they can deceive all but the most discerning eye.

As Christians, we need to pray for discernment, in order to see these evil people and destroy their works before they are allowed to wreak havoc in our lives.

In I Corinthian 12:7-10, we find that among the gifts that the Holy Spirit gives to believers is the *discerning of spirits*. And in 1 John 4:1, we are warned to believe not every spirit, but to "*try the spirits whether they are of God: because many false prophets are gone out into the world. Hereby know ye the Spirit of God: Every spirit that confesseth that Jesus Christ is come in the flesh is of God: And every spirit that confesseth not that Jesus Christ is come in the flesh is not of God: and this is that spirit of antichrist, whereof ye have heard that it should come; and even now already is it in the world.*"

In the next chapter, we'll come to understand how to destroy the works of darkness.

CHAPTER THREE:

ENTERING INTO THE BATTLE

After five years of walking with the Lord, I had done a little growing, gained a little wisdom, and made many mistakes. However, the Lord blessed me to be able to correct the mistakes.

I met one lady that asked me to be her mother in the Lord. I told her that I would help her as much as I could. So, I took her in, as a friend, praying with her many times and fasting with her over a two-year period.

Within those two years, many strange things started happening to me, for instance: I was working on the dock loading a van when a forklift being driven back-and-forth, almost hit me. The forklift passed by me four times, and each time, the driver lost control and nearly hit me. I asked him, "What's your problem?"

He responded, "I don't know. The forklift loses control whenever it gets near you. It's doing this by itself."

I could see he was also getting pretty unnerved, so I got out of there quickly to pray. I was sensing evil.

On another day, I was loading a pallet with material at the same dock. I stopped for a minute to take a break. As I as standing there, a strong force pushed me backwards and I began to fall. There was nothing to grab on to. If I had fallen, I would have landed head-first on the concrete below. But, apparently the angels pushed me back up.

"For he shall give his angels charge over thee, to keep thee in all thy ways. They shall bear thee up in their hands, lest thou dash thy foot against a stone."
(Psalm 91:11-12)

A co-worker witnessed the incident. He, of course, was very puzzled, but since he was unsaved, he couldn't understand. I then told him about the forklift incident, which just added to his confusion.

At other times, I'd be driving along when suddenly cars on the opposite side of the street began losing control. The cars would go out of control, as if attempting to hit me head on. I'd call on the name of Jesus. Then, they would swerve back just in the nick of time. Or, I'd be walking and lose my breath, causing my heart to palpitate. I had a good, healthy heart, so there was no logical reason for this happening.

I began to seek the Lord about what was happening and the Lord showed me in a dream the friend I prayed with for two years. She was standing over my bed dressed in black. Then, in another dream, I was walking with her and I kept falling, holding my chest. Again, she was dressed in black.

The Lord revealed to me that she was working witchcraft, and trying to kill me. That's when I confronted her about these dreams. I was expecting her to deny it, but she confessed. And, she said that since I loved Jesus so much I shouldn't mind going home to be with Him. She wanted my "anointing" to fall upon her. I immediately dissolved our friendship hoping that these episodes would now quickly come to an end. But they didn't.

An evil presence would come around me when I'd try to sleep and when I'd pray. I was constantly being attacked. I discerned that it was coming from her. So, I began to pray against the powers of witchcraft and their works. Periodically, the evil presence would go away for a while, then later come back. It was revealed to me that she was fasting to make her powers stronger. Therefore, I went on a three-day fast and prayed completely through, never allowing her name to come out of my mouth, but just breaking the powers of witchcraft coming against me. And, it ceased.

But she went and told her pastor that I was praying evil prayers against her. Her pastor approached me about her statement. I simply told the pastor that I did not pray evil prayers against anyone but that I just broke the powers of witchcraft in the name of Jesus. I said, "If there are evil things happening to her it is because her own evil works have backfired on her."

Afterwards, each time I'd fast, I'd pray and ask God to bless and strengthen the discernment of spirits within me. The following Scripture came to me:

"The light of the body is the eye: if therefore thine eye be single, thy whole body shall be full of light. But if thine eye be evil, thy whole body shall be full of darkness. If therefore the light that in thee be darkness, how great is that darkness!"

(St. Matthew 6:22-23)

Now, based on this Scripture, when I meet and speak with others, I make full contact with their eyes. Over a period of time, God has also blessed me, through the gift of discernment, with the ability to see, hear, feel and smell the presence of demonic activities.

Another incident occurred when I met a lady who was an ex-devil worshipper, a high priestess, who had been born again, washed in the blood and filled with the Holy Spirit. She was telling me about how she had an operation six month's prior. She said that the wound wouldn't heal because a nurse-witch stood over her in the hospital and had chanted. While I was talking with her over the phone, I told her to put her right hand on the wound and pray. I prayed in the name of Jesus, and commanded the powers of witchcraft to be broken and destroyed. Then, I asked Jesus to loose healing to that wound. I checked with her two months later, and she told me the wound had closed and was healing beautifully.

Shortly afterwards, a great presence of evil surrounded my house and I had terrible headaches every day. I tried to find out from various ministers what was going on. Ministers can be really good at avoiding a situation when they want to do so. They suggested that it was all in my mind. But I forgave them.

One minister told me that there was no power that strong. One day, he came over to my house to pray for me and his head was attacked with one of the worst headaches he'd ever had. The headache felt like there was a vice-grip around his head. He said that he, "had never seen anything like this," and quickly left.

I called my cousin who is a pastor in Southern California, and he pointed out to me that this attack was a result of praying for the ex-witch's healing. He told me to just keep on fasting and praying.

One day, I was at a church in the Danville/Dublin California area. While I was at the altar praying, the pastor began to minister to me saying, "Sister, there is a flock of demons around your house. They are there to destroy you, but God is not going to let it be so. He is going to deliver you. There is a great work that God will have you to do in the area of coming against the powers of darkness."

This minister didn't know me, nor could he have known what I was going through. So, that was a word from the Lord, and it was a great encouragement to me.

I continued seeking the Lord, and the Lord instructed me while I was fasting and praying that I should put my prayer sessions on tape. And, so, I did. I let the tape play for twenty-four hours a day. I continued to pray and the headache broke. Also, the evil forces departed from my house.

The prayers that God had given me consisted of destroying the works of witchcraft, paralyzing chanting and evil spirits by praying in my heavenly language, and breaking every spell. Also, I prayed that the demonic spirits would be confused in their wisdom, in the name of Jesus.

I was in this battle alone. I looked for someone to pray with me, but no one did. Maybe if someone had prayed with me, it would have hindered my instructions from the Lord or I could have become dependent upon that person. God knows. God knows why I walked this battle alone. Of course, Jesus won in this battle and I learned how to battle witchcraft through this experience.

Another time, as I was driving down a street in my city I passed a church. The Lord told me to go into that church, for their ministry had been under heavy attack from witchcraft. So, I visited the church to speak with the pastor. I told him why God had sent me, and I told him about the witchcraft coming against his church. He agreed and welcomed me there to pray.

I went to the church and began to intercede with fasting and prayer, using the knowledge that God had given me. As a result, the spirit of God began to flow, and the pastor also began flowing under a great anointing. The church began to grow.

Just when we thought everything was okay, more witches and warlocks started coming to the church. One Sunday morning, I walked into the church and got sick to my stomach. Then, I broke out in a sweat. I walked out, and the Lord instructed me to go on a twenty-one-day fast.

I called the pastor the next day and told him that I would be home fasting and conducting warfare for twenty-one days because the witches had gotten reinforcements. The pastor agreed. He said that after he would preach, he'd feel very drained. This meant that the evil power had gotten stronger. He also said that he'd sleep for twelve hours every night and would still have to fight to get out of bed. I told him not to tell anyone where I was, or what I was doing. I wanted the witches and the warlocks to think that they had run me off.

While praying at home, the Lord showed me visions and instructed me how to pray and how to speak to the demonic forces that were carrying out the witchcraft against the pastor and the church. I prayed as follows: "You demons of witchcraft, curses and spells, in the name of Jesus, your powers and strength are destroyed, and from this day forth, you shall not touch or hinder Pastor _____ or _____ Church." I sealed the words with the blood of Jesus. Then, I would pray in my heavenly language and continue praying until I got a complete breakthrough. I did this for twenty-one days, singing praises and glorifying God.

After completing the twenty-one day fast, I walked into Pastor _____'s office. He was glowing, bubbly and full of joy. And, he said, "Sister, come here. Let me tell you what the Lord has done." He said that all the witches that he was aware of, had left the church, except for one. And, that she had repented and confessed. He also said that he had been receiving revelation knowledge, after revelation knowledge, after revelation knowledge. This minister is now pastoring four to five thousand members.

The Lord led me to warfare against witches and attacks upon several other churches, that I will not discuss at this time. But, in the experience of engaging in warfare, I learned how to fight against the strong demons assisting the witches and warlocks.

"For the weapons of our warfare are not carnal, but mighty through God to the pulling down of strong holds."
(2 Corinthians 10:4)

Webster's New World Dictionary defines warfare, as "the act of waging war; an armed conflict or struggle of any kind." The Bible tells us that we are in a battle and that we must put on the whole armour of God. That we are not battling against flesh or blood and that the weapons we use are not tangible. Our enemy is unseen, and we fight him and his demons with the Word of God, which is the sword of the Spirit (Ephesians 6:11-17), by prayer and fasting (Matthew 17:21), the blood of the Lamb and our Christian testimony (Revelations 12:11).

Although it is covered in the Word, many saints don't understand that there are ranks of demons in the heavenlies. Ephesians 6:12 lists these levels as *"principalities, powers, rulers of the darkness of this world, spiritual wickedness in high places."* The Lord taught me that these demons assist witches and empower them to do evil.

Several months later, I was laying in my bed with my back to the bedroom door. I was reading when suddenly the Holy Ghost said, "Look over your shoulder." I looked and saw a dragon, eyes piercing and wicked, looking at me with an evil glare. I began to say repeatedly, "Jesus! Jesus! Jesus!" When I had said, "Jesus" three times, the dragon disappeared. Part of my body was just as cold as if it had been in an icebox. I continued saying, "Jesus" until my body temperature returned to normal.

Once again, I give God the praise and the glory, for fear did not come upon me. I knew this was the peace of the Lord Jesus keeping me.

"Ye are of God, little children, and have overcome them: because greater is He that is within you than he that is in the world."

(1 John 4:4 KJV)

Another time, I was driving through Southern California, coming back from a Christian meeting accompanied by three other people. Suddenly a pick-up truck came up close to my rearend as if it was going to ram me. I began to say, "Satan, in the name of Jesus, I bind and destroy your works."

Then, the pick-up immediately pulled around me on the passenger's side and the driver glared into my window. His eyes were cold, dark and piercing; his face was white, very pale and fangs were hanging out of his mouth. Once again, I said, "In the name of Jesus, I bind you, you devil." And, he took off.

To God be the glory for another victorious moment. I do believe that these were the schemes of Satan to try to make me back off. But the more he schemed, the more Christ arose in me which gave me even more determination to do the will of God. For as long as I stay in the will of God, Satan can only do what God gives him permission to do and no more.[1]

---

[1]   I stayed in this battle for about a year. Thank God for the victory.

CHAPTER FOUR:

WINNING THE BATTLE

As I was praying before the Lord, God spoke to me. He told me to go to a certain city to intercede and conduct warfare for a church whose ministry was under a very heavy attack. (Intercession, defined in *Unger's Concise Bible Dictionary*, is a form of prayer in which the petitioner stands between God and some great need. Read Romans 8:26-27.)

I said, "Okay, Lord." And I went. I approached the pastor after the service and told him that I had come to do warfare against the witches and warlocks that were attacking his ministry.

One witch and a warlock somehow knew the purpose for which I was there, and they began to wage war against me. All kinds of demonic activity and forces were coming toward me. My car kept breaking down to prevent me getting to the church. I'd wake up coughing and choking. A strong-smelling scent of sulfur mixed with another indescribable odor entered my nostrils while I slept; and I would wake up doing battle.

The power would be broken for a season, then it would come back, over and over again. This went on from the month of December until about the end of March in the following year.

I began to fast, pray, and ask God why this battle kept going back and forth. Then, the Lord asked me, "What makes a Christian successful?" And, I replied, "The Spirit of Christ that lives within him."

"To whom God would make known what is the riches of the glory of this mystery among the Gentiles; which is Christ in you, the hope of glory."
(Colossians 1:27 KJV)

"And," I also replied to the Lord, "having the works of faith."

"Wherefore also we pray always for you, that our God would count you worthy of this calling, and fulfill all the good pleasure of his goodness, and the work of faith with power: That the name of our Lord Jesus Christ may be glorified in you, and ye in him, according to the grace of our God and the Lord Jesus Christ."
(II Thessalonians 1:11-12 KJV)

At the church, while on my knees praying, the Lord began to reveal to me what makes witches, warlocks, and devil-worshippers successful in their works. They are driven by **fear, hate, greed** and **pride.**

Immediately, I began to pray and curse the powers and the works of fear, hate, greed and pride along with murder, wizardry, and sorcery - in the name of Jesus - destroying their very works and preventing these spirits from operating in that person yielded to Satan. Also, in the name of Jesus, I silenced the spirit guides and cursed the spirit of blindness, heaviness and bondage. I asked God to open up that person's eyes that he may see the glory of Jesus, and open up the ear of his heart that he may hear the Lord's voice. I prayed that the Lord would reveal to that person all the evil that he was doing, so that his heart would come under conviction. I wanted him to come to repentance.

> "He hath blinded their eyes, and hardened their heart; that they should not see with their eyes, nor understand with their heart, and be converted, and I should heal them."
>
> (St. John 12:40 KJV)

> "For ye have not received the spirit of bondage again to fear; but ye have received the Spirit of adoption, whereby we cry, Abba, Father."
>
> (Romans 8:15 KJV)

Shortly afterwards, the warlock made a complete change. The hardness of heart left, and a softness began to appear upon him. He openly confessed that he was into satanism, and that he had killed people by putting curses on them. He admitted to working through witchcraft sex, and many kinds of pagan rituals. He also stopped walking back-and-forth during the church services, and began to really participate in the praising and worshipping.

I want to emphasize that if these devils and their works are destroyed in a person, then they will no longer be successful in working witchcraft against the church and the children of God. By the way, the witch became so powerless at that church that she eventually left.

I had said, "Lord, this is very simple. We just need to fast and pray, and destroy the works of **fear, hate, greed** or **whatever stronghold** is driving a witch, warlock, sorcerer or high priest." From that point on, my battles against any witch, warlock or any similar form of evil agent became much easier. I'd simply go on a small three-day fast to find out which evil characteristic was dominant in that person, and then begin to pray.

Remember, witches and warlocks are human beings. So, without the devils operating in them, they are not going to be successful. As the Scripture indicated, in the case of Jesus casting out the devil, called Legion, when the devil left, the man was restored to his right mind.

"When he saw Jesus, he cried out, and fell down before him, and with a loud voice said, What have I to do with thee, Jesus, thou Son of God most high? I beseech thee, torment me not. (For he had commanded the unclean spirit to come out of the man. For oftentimes it had caught him: and he was kept bound with chains and in fetters; and he brake the bands, and was driven of the devil into the wilderness). And Jesus asked him, saying, What is thy name? And he said, Legion: because many devils were entered into him. And they besought him that he would not command them to go out into the deep. And there was there an herd of many swine feeding on the mountain: and they besought him that he would suffer them to enter into them. And he suffered them. Then went the devils out of the man, and entered into the swine: and the herd ran violently down a steep place into the lake, and were choked. When they that fed them saw what was done, they fled, and went and told it in the city and in the country. Then they went out to see what was done; and came to Jesus, and found the man, out of whom the devils were departed, sitting at the feet of Jesus, clothed, and in his right mind: and they were afraid."

(St. Luke 8:28-35 KJV)

There was another Christian meeting to which the Lord drew me, and blessed me by calling me into warfare. I spoke with a lady who had been working with the ministry and explained to her that I wanted to come in and intercede against the powers of darkness and witchcraft. She gave me a counselor's badge, so that I could enter the building and do warfare right before each meeting. I would arrive hours before the meeting began. Then I'd go into an area where I wouldn't draw attention to myself and begin to intercede and conduct warfare, in the name of Jesus, against the powers of darkness. These devils were forbidden, in the name of Jesus, to interfere with the witches, so that they would be able to make a free will decision to receive Jesus and get saved.

The prayer was as follows: *"In the name of Jesus, Satan, you and all your influences and hindering spirits are totally paralyzed and totally forbidden from hindering these witches and warlocks from making up their own minds to give their lives to the Lord. They will have their own free will choice to come to the Lord. So, you are totally silenced, in the name of Jesus."* Then, I would pray through in my heavenly language until I received a breakthrough. Once this occurred, I knew that it was done.

An usher that travels regularly with the ministry came up to me as I finished praying. She asked what I had been praying for. I told her that I was praying for the witches present to be saved. She looked at me, nodded her head and went on. That Friday night, the minister stopped and said that there was one witch in the service that the Lord wanted to save. He called for one, and then many other witches came to the altar. Later, at a different meeting, the same usher told me that she was a witness that I had conducted effective warfare for the witches to be saved, and that she had also witnessed the results.

Another time, in another city, she said, "I travel around to a lot of these meetings and I have never seen anything like what happened with the witches, ever!" It wasn't I that did the warfaring, but it was the Christ who lives in me. To God be the glory!

On a different occasion, I went to a conference and God instructed me to go on a seven-day-and-night fast.

He instructed me to warfare before each meeting. And, so, I quietly went in before each service, and would either get on my knees or sit and pray to intercede and do warfare against the powers of darkness that were operating in the witches. There were many of them at that particular meeting.[2] After praying, there was no heaviness or interference from them at all, and God reigned. Also, other people attending had indicated that there were a lot of witches at that particular meeting, but still, there was no interference from them. They were powerless!

Again, I was there to intercede and bind up the powers, and destroy the works of all the witches in each meeting. In the name of Jesus, the spirit guides were forbidden to come into the meeting. There is so much power in the name of Jesus alone; a tremendous amount of power. By the way, one can easily warfare in different meetings quietly, without drawing attention to oneself. That way, no one even knows what you're doing, and God gets all the glory.

---

[2] Many times, witches, etc. have not been truly loved, or they have been hurt, misused and abused by their parents or someone in their childhood. Many of them may even have come to the Christian church and been again rejected. But the church of darkness would receive them with open arms! The Christian church needs to be careful about showing the love of Christ to all people, regardless of how they look. God is love!

"Reproach hath broken my heart; and I am full of heaviness: and I looked for some to take pity, but there was none; and for comforters, but I found none."   (Psalms 69:20 KJV)

There is an example in Scripture of a certain damsel possessed with a spirit of divination.

"And it came to pass, as we went to prayer, a certain damsel possessed with a spirit of divination met us, which brought her masters much gain by soothsaying: The same followed Paul and us, and cried, saying, These men are the servants of the most high God, which shew unto us the way of salvation. And this did she many days. But Paul, being grieved, turned and said to the spirit, I command thee in the name of Jesus Christ to come out of her. And he came out the same hour."

(Acts 16:16-18 KJV)

This again illustrates that once the evil works were destroyed the person became powerless.

* * *

THE WAY I PRAY

"In the Name of ***Jesus Christ of Nazareth,*** *I come against the prince-ruling spirit and all spirit guides. I come through the blood of the Lord Jesus Christ, in the Name of Jesus. I paralyze you and silence you, forbidding you from influencing or strengthening them (the witch or witches) in the Name of Jesus, right now!*

We are destroying your very works: the spirits of hate, bitterness and murder, spirits of wizardry, sorcery and all your co-spirits, your works, your powers, your influences are destroyed in the Name of Jesus!

I paralyze you, all, right now. You will not be able to use this soul any longer against the church (or, a particular person), in the Name of Jesus.

I come against the spirit of blindness, binding the spirits of bondage and heaviness, fear and hate.

I pray, Lord, that You will open their eyes so they can see the glory of Jesus. Open their hearts so that they can hear Your voice. Break the yokes in their lives and give them liberty in their souls, that they may be free to repent. Show them every evil work and every evil deed they're guilty of, and Lord Jesus, convict their hearts unto repentance. Bring these souls out of darkness; save these souls so that You may have the glory.

Satan, I silence you in the name of Jesus, binding all your interference. You will not interfere with these souls and they will have their own free will choice so as to make up their own minds if they want to repent. They will do it without your interference.

Also, Lord, I pray that you will release warring angels to wage war against these demonic activities, and will send ministering spirits to minister to their souls."

After praying in this way, I then start praying in the Spirit "with groanings which cannot be uttered" (Romans 8:26), until the Holy Spirit begins to intercede, leading me into deep travail. I keep praying, praying, praying, until I get a breakthrough in the spirit realm. When I get in the spirit realm, then I know the Lord is working. Even if an individual witch doesn't repent, she (or he) becomes powerless and unsuccessful in hindering a church, a family, a person, or a marriage.

CONCLUSION

Many years ago, God awoke me one evening and told me, "Ruthie, the church is asleep and the occult world is rapidly increasing." It is time for the saints to wake up, put on their battle garments, and fight the forces of darkness.

"He that committeth sin is of the devil; for the devil sinneth from the beginning. For this purpose the Son of God was manifested, that he might destroy the works of the devil."
(1 John 3:8)

I'd like to advise those who are warfaring against the powers of darkness to please fast and pray, and ask God to first show you your own weakness. For, it is important for you first to be delivered. If you aren't delivered, Satan will use your own weakness against you and you'll become your own worst enemy. Although I mentioned this in an earlier chapter, I feel strongly the need to repeat this statement.

Before beginning a fast, I'd advise everyone to get a good herbal laxative, to help clean out your system. This will prevent the food poisons and toxins from attacking your body, giving you headaches, and generally making you sluggish and irritable.

Sometimes Satan will attempt to fight you at the beginning of your fast in an effort to hinder you. But press on your way, as Philippians 3:14 states:

"I press toward the mark for the prize of the high calling of God in Christ Jesus."

It's always a great blessing when you manage to press through to the end of the fast. Lots of times the fast will both prepare you and take you through any temptations that do come upon you. It will also sharpen your spiritual awareness and enable you to warfare successfully against the enemy.

Daniel was seeking to understand the vision which he had received of the latter days. He was mourning three full weeks and ate no pleasant bread or flesh until the three weeks were fulfilled. The angel appeared and said unto him:

"Fear not, Daniel: for from the first day that thou didst set thine heart to understand, and to chasten thyself before thy God, thy words were heard, and I am come for thy words. But the prince of the kingdom of Persia withstood me one and twenty days: but, lo, Michael, one of the chief princes, came to help me; and I remained there with the kings of Persia."

(Daniel 10:12-13)

The enemy will try to stop or hinder the blessings of God from getting to you. But remember, fasting will put wings on your prayer and will get results in the spirit world.

Please seek God for the type and length of fast that you should undertake before beginning the fast.

"In all thy ways acknowledge him, and he shall direct thy paths."

(Proverbs 3:6)

Some God may lead on a dry fast, others with water, and others with juice. It all depends on your body, and on what God wants to accomplish.

Go into fasting with the right motives: not for selfish reasons or personal gain, but rather to seek God, His kingdom, and His will for your life. If it's done properly the fasting and prayer will bring great anointing into your life.

"And it shall come to pass in that day, that his burden shall be taken away from off thy shoulder, and his yoke from off thy neck, and the yoke shall be destroyed because of the anointing."

Isaiah 10:27

Jesus said that we are to not only do the same works that He did, but also greater works. We know that He defeated the enemy at Calvary, however, evil works are still occurring in our land. Jesus gave us the power to walk and tread upon serpents, and also to destroy the works of our enemy. Churches should not have to be defeated by evil works, neither should individual Christians. The finances of the body of Christ should also not be in a state of defeat. Remember, *we have already won through Christ Jesus!*

Many witches and warlocks have come to the Lord without getting grounded in the deeper things of God, and been placed in positions of leadership in the church. Yet, the Word of God says, "He that has a ministry, let him wait upon it." (Romans 12:7)

You have to be made and molded for your ministry. You also have to be tested and tried, and go through the fire. So, I would caution pastors to wait upon the Lord and to really seek God before ordaining people and putting them into responsible positions shortly after getting saved. Many souls have been destroyed because they were advanced too quickly.

"Not a novice, lest being lifted up with pride he fall into the condemnation of the devil."

I Timothy 3:6

The church must wake up. It must arise and take its victorious position in Christ. God has given us the power to destroy all the works of witchcraft through fasting and prayer, in the Name of Jesus!

MAY GOD BLESS YOU ALL!

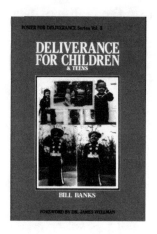

DELIVERANCE FOR CHILDREN & TEENS

The first practical handbook for ministering deliverance to children.

The material in this book is arranged to help parents in diagnosing their children's problems and in finding solutions for destructive behavior patterns.

The **Doorways** section of this book illustrates how demons enter, and how they take advantage of innocent, vulnerable children. More than a dozen categories of routes of entry are identified, and examples given!

The section on **Discipline** will be especially helpful to parents who wish to avoid problems, or remove them before they can become entrenched.

The **Mechanics of Ministry** section will help you, step by step, in ministering to a child needing help.

You will learn simple, surprising truths. For example...
* Easiest of all ministry is to small children! * Discipline is the most basic form of spiritual warfare and can bring deliverance!
* A child can acquire demonic problems through heredity or personal experience! * Deliverance need not be frightening if properly presented!

$6.95, Plus $1.50 Shipping

IMPACT CHRISTIAN BOOKS, INC.
332 Leffingwell Avenue, Suite 101
Kirkwood, MO 63122

EXCITING NEW BOOK
ANSWERS AGE-OLD QUESTION

The author draws upon the Scriptural patterns and keys established by the Prophet Daniel to present readily understandable methods any believer can employ to *Tap into the Wisdom of God*. He shows from Scripture that it is both God's intention and will for man to turn to Him as the Source of knowledge.

You will learn seven major keys to receiving knowledge and find at least twenty-one practical encouragements to build your faith to seek God for answers.

Plus a Revelation

Discover for yourself the fascinating and prophetic secrets contained in Daniel Chapter Six, presented in the ninth chapter of this book. Chapter nine, which is actually a bonus book, presents an apparently undiscovered revelation showing more than one hundred parallels between Daniel and Jesus Christ.

"The most exciting thing I discovered was that what God did for Daniel, He can do for any believer!"
P.M., Bible Teacher, Kansas.

$10.95 + $1.50 Shipping

Impact Christian Books, Inc.
332 Leffingwell Ave., Suite 101,
Kirkwood, MO 63122

Bestseller!!

PIGS IN THE PARLOR $7.95

If you *really believe* JESUS delivered people from evil spirits . . . Then you owe it to yourself to read this book! Learn that it *still happens today!*

This book contains a wealth of practical information for the person **interested in, planning to engage in, or actively engaged in** the ministry of deliverance.

It is a PRACTICAL HANDBOOK, offering valuable guidance as to determining . . .

> ● **HOW DEMONS ENTER** ● **IF DELIVERANCE IS NEEDED** ● **HOW DELIVERANCE IS ACCOMPLISHED FOR OTHERS AND SELF** ● **HOW TO RETAIN DELIVERANCE** ● **GROUPINGS OF DEMONS** (listing those demons that are often found together).

The book also includes a chapter presenting a revelation on the problems of **SCHIZOPHRENIA** which could well revolutionize the way this subject has been traditionally viewed by the medical profession!

Impac **Chris** **tian** **Books**

332 Leffingwell Ave., Suite 101
Kirkwood, MO 63122

AVAILABLE AT YOUR LOCAL BOOKSTORE, OR YOU MAY
ORDER DIRECTLY. Toll-Free, order-line only M/C, DISC,
or VISA 1-800-451-2708.

Visit our Website at *www. impactchristianbooks.com*

Write for *FREE* Catalog.